THE 4 WEEK AGENCY

*The proven step by step process
to help you start a successful
online business from home*

By Robert Hunter

DEDICATION

To my father Everard Hunter, who sadly passed away in March 2019 and my incredible Step Mother Anne, who sadly passed away in April 2019. Both of you shaped me into the man I am today and losing you both so soon into starting my business motivated me to make it the success it is today. I hope you are looking down and I have made you proud.

CONTENTS

ACKNOWLEDGMENTS

I would just like to start by saying thank you to my incredible partner Bethany, without her in my life I would probably still be lost, unhappy and without anywhere to call home. This is your book just as much as it is mine as it wouldn't have been possible without your contributions.

I would next like to thank some of my closest friends Danny, Ellis & Khiry for supporting me the last 10 years while I struggled to find my place in the world. I hope the next 10 years we can grow and build incredible lives as you all deserve it.

I would also like to mention my parents who are no longer here with me anymore, losing you last year was the hardest thing I have ever had to go through but i've come out of the other side a million times stronger and I am just getting started!

Finally I just want to thank my family members who have supported me by providing me a home and support during the years I didn't have a penny to my name or any idea how the real world works. Thank you Matthew, Marie, Troy, J, Eva, Rio and everyone else who helped me become the man I am today. I love you all dearly.

INTRODUCTION

When I dropped out of college at 17 I had no idea what I wanted to do with my life and had no role models to show me the way to a successful career. My parents were both former drug addicts who basically never worked a legal job in their lives and had spent the duration of my life on benefits struggling to get by each month.

Coming from such humble beginnings my dad always hoped I would find a good job and save up enough money to get myself a house one day but with no qualifications or connections around me, finding a great career felt like an impossible job especially after all my friends left me to go to university.

Not long after dropping out of college, I was searching for the best ways to become successful on Youtube and I came across a film about the law of attraction called *The Secret*, and instantly I started to feel like I knew what direction I wanted my life to go in.

After seeing all these people in the film who had visualised their dream life and then focused on it daily until they achieved their goal, I quickly realised I didn't just want a boring career that pays me the same amount of money every year in exchange for most of my time every single week.

I had always seen people online that were making a lot of money from their laptops and traveling the world and that seemed like the most exciting thing I could possibly do! So, I quickly decided this was what I wanted to do with my life... Become an online entrepreneur!

The problem I had was I didn't know a single thing about business and up until the age of 18, I didn't actually know what marketing was. I had no experience when it came to doing anything to do with making money or even how to sell something.

I knew I had a long way to go if I was ever going to be successful and so I became obsessed with studying business-related topics. I didn't have any mentors or role models around me to teach me how to be successful, so I decided I would learn as much as I could about how people make money online through books and you-tube videos.

Being broke and working part-time jobs to cover living expenses meant that I couldn't afford online courses or even full price books, so I spent hours every week going to charity shops in the hopes of finding a good business book for £1.

Eventually, I had collected hundreds of books and did my best to read as much as I could while always watching any business train-ing videos I could get my hands on. The crazy thing was the more I studied business the further away from being ready to start I felt.

There were so many different ways people had become rich on-line from their businesses that I just didn't know which one would be right for me. I tried:

- Trading Stocks
- Affiliate marketing
- Email marketing
- Starting a membership site
- Creating online courses
- Becoming a YouTuber
- Becoming a blogger

After trying all these and more I started to feel like starting your own online business was actually a scam and it was nearly impos-sible for 99% of the world. That was until I learned 1 valuable les-son that completely changed the way I looked at business.

Starting a successful business has much less to do with creating a business idea that you can simply start quickly and make money from and much more to do with providing more value to your customer base than the customer provides to you. If your number one focus is to make money, your business will fail.

There are thousands of ways to make money online but whichever way you choose to make money, you need to make sure you are providing more value to the customer than you are taking. People are willing to pay £1000 for the latest iPhone because they feel that they are getting more than £1000 in value from the phone. We spend £25 on a meal at a restaurant because the food, time saved cooking and experience is worth more than the money spent on the meal.

Now that I knew I had to stop thinking about myself and how I could get rich quick without putting in any effort, I needed to find a business where I could provide value to people without having any money to start and would still pay me enough to quit my job and work for myself full time.

I tried many different businesses such as creating my own online store dropshipping products from China but these stores rapidly failed as nobody wants to wait weeks for their products and you realistically need a few thousand pounds in the bank to get started advertising your store.

I also tried a membership group where I gave customers daily horse racing tips but unfortunately, horse racing is very hard to get right all the time and there were too many bad periods that made the service nearly impossible to succeed.

It wasn't until I was a victim of an armed robbery at work that I decided enough was enough and it was time for me to figure out the best business to start and finally make it happen. I was so sick of waking up at 07:00am each day wanting to cry because I didn't want to go to work and waste my life for £7 an hour when I knew I was capable of so much more!

A few days after the robbery I booked a 1-way ticket to Tenerife which was my first ever holiday at the age of 23 and I promised myself that I wouldn't come back until I had finally started the first business that would actually change my life.

During my time away I discovered online marketing agencies and I instantly fell in love with the business and how everything worked. I studied as much as I could and then announced to the world that I had started my own Marketing Agency for small businesses.

At first, I just focused on social media content but quickly learned that it's impossible for business owners to tell how much money I was helping them make from my posts, so my clients would stop working with me within 3 months as they were wasting money.

So then I made the switch from social media posts to running Facebook advertising for local businesses but this proved to be just as hard for different reasons. At the time I was low in confidence and only approached tiny businesses that could barely afford to pay out £100 a month. This meant that I was unable to get much experience or skills with Facebook as Advertising isn't cheap and if you don't know what you are doing you can quickly waste the client's money.

While struggling with my 1 remaining client at the time, I was given the opportunity by a family friend to talk to a successful online clothing store about helping them with their social media. I was honestly rubbish at online marketing at this point and this business was making £100,000 a month so I really struggled to think how I could help them with my limited skills.

Their social media and their advertising were so much better than anything I could ever do so how could I make the most of this chance and convince them to give me an opportunity to work with them?

The answer… Email marketing.

After doing a little research I quickly began to realise that a lot of online businesses were neglecting to focus on creating a good email marketing strategy for their business. Often this was because they were too focused on the more popular and sexy ways of making sales such as Facebook ads and Instagram Influencers. Most online stores understood the importance of email but very few actually understand how to make the money from email marketing because they are so busy with all the other tasks involved in running an online store.

Email is so important to an online business because when a customer gives you their email address you can now legally advertise your products to them anytime you like for free. Not only that but you can build a relationship with that customer through personalised content and discounts, unlike Facebook where you are limited to what you can share based on their guidelines.

On average a business with a good email marketing strategy can increase their monthly sales by up to 40% so this instantly made sense to me as the perfect service to start to offer to people moving forward.

After meeting with the £100k a month brand, I convinced them to let me manage their email marketing for £500 a month which at the time was a huge ask considering I had little evidence I could help them increase the £4000 a month they were currently making from email marketing.

After a slow start with a small amount of growth for the first 2 months, I had started to get the hang of email marketing and how to consistently get results. Before I knew it I was making them £10,000 a month, then £20,000, and then fast forward 18 months later we just made £120,000 in a single month from email.

As the months went on and my skills improved this client recommended me to 2 other people who owned successful brands who needed email marketing. Things went well with them and for a year or so I was managing 3-4 clients at a time making around £1200 a month which was more than I used to make in my minimum wage jobs so I was happy enough working an hour a day and just chilling each month.

For a while, I got comfortable in a routine of minimal work and effort and forgot that the goal of running a business is to keep growing it to a point where you could hire people and make life-changing money.

It wasn't until one of my clients went from making £200,000 a month to £30,000 a month during the start of the Coronavirus pandemic and had to let me go that reality started to sink in. I realised I had to get my act together and take this business seriously in case I lost my other 3 clients and was forced to get a job that I worked so hard to escape from.

That same day I began searching Instagram for online clothing stores with whom I could possibly target with my service and I began emailing as many as I could with the same copy and pasted message in the hopes that somebody would reply. Luckily for me, this was the start of my life beginning to change forever.

Over the next few days, a few brand owners got back to me and after a phone call explaining how I could help their business, I started to get clients with relative ease. Within a month I went from £850 a month and 3 clients to £2000 a month and 8 clients. Not quite life-changing money but £24,000 a year just to stay at home and work 2 hours a day doing something I loved felt like a blessing to me.

Just as things were starting to look up and I thought I could relax, I got the news I had always feared but expected to come eventually...My first and biggest paying client was hiring someone to manage their emails and other jobs as a full-time employee. I was initially gutted having helped take their emails from £4000 to £120,000 a month but I knew they had reached a point where they were so big I was no longer needed.

About to lose out on 25% of my monthly income I knew I had to level up again and get more clients on board. Not only that, but I had made over £1 million in sales for clients while only charging 1% of what I made them each month, it was time for me to increase my prices.

My biggest client agreed to pay me for my final month's work which meant I had until the end of the month to replace the £500 I was about to lose each month. Using all the methods I had used in the past to get clients, I quickly replaced that client's monthly fee 5X over within a few weeks and was now making £4000 a month which is something I thought would never happen.

I had completely changed my business to be as efficient and profitable as possible by removing my smaller clients who were taking up a lot of my time for small amounts of money like £100 a month. My job was basically the same for £1000 clients as it was for £100 a month clients who typically made me work harder because they found it harder to make sales as their business wasn't very successful yet. I replaced these time-wasting clients with higher quality clients that could afford higher fees because they were already making money but were not focused on email marketing.

Fast forward to today and the results for my clients are better than ever and I have hired people onto my team to help my agency grow into the number 1 email marketing agency in the UK in 2021.

It took me 8 years to build ,y first successful online business that allowed me to work from home and be in full control of my life. My goal with this book is to show you everything I have learned during my journey of many failures and successes. I want to give you the step by step blueprint to starting and managing your first successful agency within the next 4 weeks.

This book is filled with the exact business model and strategies

I use to get business owners I have never even met before to pay me up to £1000 a month to do something that only takes me a few hours a week to achieve consistent results. There are many different types of online agencies you can start today that would get you great results and sales, email marketing works for me but in later chapters, we will discuss all the other agencies you could start that may suit you better.

1. WHY YOU SHOULD START AN AGENCY

Never in the history of mankind has there been a better time for you to start your first online business. The world was quickly taking everything online before 2020 but ever since the start of the Covid-19 pandemic the rate at which online business sales have grown has been massive. Many high street businesses are being forced to either close down or go online to survive.

As the demand to buy things online increases worldwide the demand for people who have the skills to help online businesses make more money also increases. Regular jobs that people have done for years such as shop cashiers have been replaced by machines and non-essential jobs will only continue to become increasingly harder to find as more and more people lose their careers.

Businesses will always be able to replace a cashier or other non-essential workers, but what they can't replace is a marketer or advertiser that consistently helps their business get customers and make more sales. Now you could do the traditional thing and look on job finding websites for companies hiring marketers and advertisers to be full-time employees but chances are you won't have the qualifications or experience they are looking for.

In my opinion, this idea would be terrible, why would you want to limit yourself to a £25,000 a year job that forces you to spend 160 hours a month helping to make your boss rich and working towards somebody else's dream?

If you started your own online agency today and got 3-4 clients you would be making the same amount of money each year while working hundreds of hours less than if you worked for somebody else.

When you go out and get a job, your employer will typically pay you based on an hourly rate. This means that whether you don't try at all or you put all your effort into a project you will always get paid the same amount each month, that you have effectively sold your soul to earn.

When you manage your own online agency from home, you control how much money you can make each month and more importantly, you are in full control of how you spend your time. Since my agency has been up and running I have been lucky enough to be able to travel the world to places like Thailand, Spain and Mexico knowing that as long as I have access to an internet connection, I will have no problem getting my work done anywhere in the world.

By the end of this book, I want you to start looking at being paid an hourly rate in the same way I do...I think hourly rates are the equivalent of modern-day slavery.

You should be paid based on the value you bring to your customers and not how much time you spend working on their business. If you help make a business £50,000 a month and it only takes you 3 hours a week, why would you charge £20 an hour just because it's a good wage when you could charge them £1000 a month as a flat fee or even £5000 a month and they would still be making £45,000 in sales that wouldn't have happened without you and your skills.

When you run your own online agency you get to charge big money fees because you are helping successful businesses become more successful. If you can save a business owner time each week and you can also help their business make more money, you are worth so much more than an hourly rate.

In the last 8 years, I have tried and experienced almost every online business model that is available and nothing compares to starting an online agency when it comes to making big profits quickly and how simple it is to start.

Most businesses require a lot of money to start up because you need to order stock, pay for advertising, staff as well as all the other hidden extras that eat away into your profits. When you manage an agency, 100% of what the client pays you will be profit, there are no costs for anything in the business other than maybe small fees to pay for your business email address and web-site.

Would you rather own an online agency making £5000 a month or an online store making £20,000 in sales a month? Personally, I would choose the agency every single time as when you take an online store's expenses into consideration they will be lucky if they are making £5000 in profit each month. While agency expenses are minimal, with an online store you have to consider the following:

- Cost of product to make
- Cost of shipping
- Hiring someone to fulfill orders
- Hiring someone to do Advertising
- Hiring someone to do Marketing
- Hiring Models
- Hiring a Photographer
- Web Hosting
- So much more!

My goal from this book is to show you how to run a business that will give you a huge profit margin with every sale and to work in the most efficient way possible so you are able to travel the world and live life with the freedom and happiness you deserve.

Not only is the profit margin per customer much higher when you have your own agency compared to an online store, once someone becomes your customer they will pay you that same amount every single month without you needing to sell anything else to them. Having a consistent amount of money coming in each month from clients is far more secure and predictable than having to sell your products to someone only for them to never come back to your store.

Having a monthly retainer is the most secure business model any business could possibly ask for as it is very hard to get customers to come back and buy from you a 2nd time no matter what industry you are in.

Inside this book is the simple step by step process that will allow you to start building a life that most people can only dream about. This isn't a long book, but it is a book filled with many powerful business lessons that I had to learn the hard way over 8 years of failing before finally succeeding.

If you follow the advice in the following chapters and take action, you have everything you need to completely change your life and start living the life I have been so fortunate to experience and want to share with the world.

2. SUCCESS REQUIREMENTS

When you are trying to start your first successful online business it can be very easy to have a lot of fears and beliefs that will stop you from being successful and have possibly prevented you from making money online in the past.

In this chapter I want to remove any myths or limiting beliefs you may have currently that might hurt your chances of starting your dream business from home. Then I want to take a deep look into who you are and what your goals are as you need to have a deep understanding of yourself and your motivations if you are going to change your life in the next few months.

Finally I will show you the number one thing that you need to focus on if you want your business to be successful, everything else can be below average if this one single aspect of your business is high quality so make sure you stay focused in this chapter.

Below are my top 10 common myths and misconceptions that people trying to start their first online business believe in and why you need to change your mindset if you also fall into any of these belief patterns below:

Money Mindset

I wanted to start off with this one because I think it's something that a lot of people especially myself have struggled with at some point. Your beliefs and understandings around money will be one of the most important factors in deciding how far your business can actually go. I often ask people what their opinions on money are, and very rarely do they say something that is positive about it, now that might be because secretly they love money but they don't want to look like a greedy person but more often than not it's because they have many limiting beliefs around money.

The main one being

Money is evil - Often i hear people say that money is evil and bad, but then I will see those same people be the tightest with money and will bring money up in every situation. We believe this narrative that all rich people are evil and greedy and should be giving their money away to the millions of less fortunate around the world but it's complete nonsense. The only way to create wealth is to provide value to the world, you cannot make a large amount of money without providing the world with something valuable that people actually want and need.

If you are working a job, and you are getting paid £10 an hour for your time... it's because the job you are doing is only worth that small £10 an hour. If you are currently only providing enough value for the world to pay you £10 for an hour of your time you need to understand why this is. It's not because this is what you are worth to the world, but that you haven't positioned yourself in the right way and taken the right action and steps to get paid what you are worth.

You can do a job as an employee who has 10 different tasks to do each and every week getting paid only £10 an hour, or you can take the 2 tasks out of those 10 that you are the best at and package that up as an exclusive service to businesses and charge £1000 for 8 hours work.

All rich people are not greedy, they just position themselves in a way that is far more valuable to the world through helpful or even entertaining products and services.

Even though there is a small amount of the wealthy population who could probably be considered "evil" their money is nothing more than a tool that they choose to use in whatever way they desire.

Look at money like a hammer or another tool, If you choose to use it correctly and wisely you can build a home, a table and many other useful and wonderful things that can benefit your life and those around you.

On the flip side, the choice could be made to use the hammer or tool for completely different purposes, like to damage, to be destructive, or to be used as a weapon and used in a robbery to strike fear into people.

The only difference in these 2 comparisons is the mindset and choices made by the person holding the hammer, the same goes for money. Money itself is nothing more than a tool...it's up to you if you want to use it for good or evil.

So learn to love and appreciate money for all the good it has done for you and you will soon find that attracting more money into your life will be far easier than ever before. You cannot have an abundance of something you hate and are subconsciously afraid of.

Entrepreneurs are born

The next limiting belief I need you to forget is the idea that the best and most successful entrepreneurs were born this way... whether it be that they are just a natural born sales person, insanely smart, insanely hard working or they were just born lucky... we love to accuse people of being blessed and naturally gifted because it's a lot easier than analysing everything these successful people did in the 10 years leading up to their success, or admitting that they did the work nobody else was willing to try for long enough to achieve that level of success.

Every famous person you see that seemingly got big overnight had to put in years and years of work behind the scenes before they reached the level of success you see them living today.

The only reason it looks like they gained success overnight is because before they got their big break nobody cared about who they were or because they only had a small circle of dedicated followers which was not enough for them to get the exposure or income required to become a household name in their industry.

Before Bill Gates became the man he is today, he spent 20 years studying and coding every single day, between the ages of 20 and 30 he never took a day off while he was building microsoft and nobody knew who he was. It wasn't until Microsoft started to have big wins that he became the man everyone knows as one of the richest people in history. He wasn't just lucky or born into success, it took 20 long and hard years to make his dreams come true.

Warren Buffet did not make his first billion until after the age of 50 and he started learning investing as a child, began investing at 12 and even found a legendary mentor in Benjamin Graham, author of The Intelligent Investor. Even though he went on to make more money than most people could ever comprehend....It still took 40+ years of hard work, reading 8 hours a day and finding great partners like Charlie Munger before he became the man we all know today.

If you look into the backstory of anyone you idolise or admire, you will see that none of them were born that way and just walked into success. It took many years of hard work and failures to shape them into the successful person they are today.

You need qualifications to get big clients and respect

This one is one of the most commonly talked about myths that I'm sure most of you would have already heard before, but this is definitely a belief you will want to remove if you feel this way currently.

On the Forbes rich list currently there are 63 people whose highest qualification comes from their secondary school. This includes Mark Zuckerberg, Bill Gates and Dustin Moskovitz. More often than not University is the best way for someone to find a good career in the industry they are passionate about but when it comes to entrepreneurship, all you need is an insane dedication to your field, mentors or training programs to guide you to the next level and the ability to understand people, persuasion and how the human mind works.

Once you know how to build a product that fixes your customer's problem, have step by step guidance and the understanding of how to persuade someone into buying anything, you have all the tools required to be ridiculously wealthy. All that remains to do is take action everyday.

No qualifications will ever help you make sales better than proven results and testimonials. If you can show evidence of your results and receive testimonials from happy customers you will make 1000x more sales with that than you ever would just because you have a fancy degree attached to your name.

Fixed Mindset

This one is very similar to entrepreneurs are born and not made, which is many people through fears and habits built over the years will believe that certain character traits they have like being lazy, sleeping late and being argumentative are just what makes up who they are and makes them unique... this couldn't be further from the truth.

The person you are and the characteristics (whether good or bad) that you have are nothing more than decisions, conscious or subconscious to be the person that acts in that way. You might be a person that has never spoken to strangers randomly in public before because you feel anxious in social situations but then after a number of years you can make the decision to become a new version of yourself who can talk to new people with ease. Of course It won't happen overnight but if you come up with the right plan of action and work at it regularly, before you know it... your fixed mindset that it was impossible to talk to new people would be eradicated and replaced with the belief that you actually love talking to new people.

If you don't believe you can change and improve as a person to become the person you want to be, you never will. People with a fixed mindset are always right because they think that what they are doing is just a part of who they are so they continue to do the same actions that keep confirming their limiting belief to themselves.

Alternatively if they decided to make a change to themselves and took daily actions towards that goal, eventually they would be proven right again but for different reasons. Instead of limiting yourself and then being happy you guessed your limits correctly...you need to have a growth mindset and understand that whatever feels like your limit is only there because you haven't got any memory or experience of what it's like to be better than you currently are. It is very possible to reach limits you couldn't even imagine if you plan correctly and take daily actions towards your goals.

New Businesses can't ask for premium rates

Another huge mistake I see almost every new business owner make is believing that due to their lack of experience and confidence that they have to charge ridiculously cheap prices for their services because they think nobody would want to buy off them if they don't make it extremely cheap to get people through the door.

New business owners are usually so desperate for their first customers that they lower their prices, their standards and the quality of their service so that they can try and convince anyone and everyone to buy from you. The problem is, if you try to cater to everyone you won't make anyone happy and they will just see your product as the cheap option that will do for now until they can afford to pay for a premium solution.

Your best strategy would be to choose a small group of people in your industry that share a similar set of problems and would require a specific tailored service created by you. Because your product would be focused on providing a tailored experience for this 1 particular type of customer you will be able to get incredible results, this means you are able to charge a lot more than you would have if you tried to help everyone. If you can provide an incredible customer experience, it doesn't matter if you are new or old... You will be able to charge premium rates. People don't buy into the product, they buy into what they think will make them feel great.

Starting a business is risky

This might have been true 20 years ago when you needed thousands of pounds to spare if you wanted to start a business, rent an office building and pay for a web designer etc. But in the modern era you can pretty much start any online business you desire for under £100. The process I am going to be showing you in this training program doesn't even require you to have a website or even a budget for advertising.

There's seriously no financial risk and while you are getting started setting up your dream business you can easily work a job and come home and continue to study the process and set up your business. If you ask me, the bigger risk would be to not start your own business... Just think about it.

If you work 40 hours a week that's 160 a month with maybe 4 weeks of holiday just to earn 20/30k a year which after rent and bills probably leaves you with around £500 to enjoy over the weekends when you don't have to work. In reality you have very little freedom and financial power to enjoy the short time you have on earth. If you manage to save £100 a month for 40 years of work you can enjoy spending your £48,000 when you retire at 65. Now if you ask me, choosing this life is a huge risk to long term happiness, legacy and mental health.

Whereas if you start the business I am going to show you in this book, you are able to change thousands of peoples lives by creating a life changing program that can make you £10,000+ a month all while working from the comfort of your own home and giving you the freedom to travel the world.

You will learn how to sell snow to eskimos, and how to always be a person of high value who can demand 100x more than you would ever earn in your job. Worst case scenario here is you fail to follow the system and you have to go back to another unsatisfying job. Best case scenario is you end up 10xing your life doing work that you enjoy waking up to each day while earning more money than ever before.

To sum up, there might be some short term risk to starting your own business but overall it is by far the most logical decision for anyone who wants to live a happy life where you are in control. It's a much bigger risk to commit to a career for 40 years and hope you can have a happy retirement.

Competition

The next limiting belief you need to remove as soon as possible is the belief that you cannot start a business if you have a lot of competition doing the same thing. This is the complete opposite of the truth! If you haven't got much competition, the chances are it's because nobody wants to buy what you're selling. Because if there is demand for something, there will always be a growing number of businesses that are starting to get a piece of the pie.

Believe it or not, the more competition you have the better opportunity you have to stand out from the crowds of screaming sales pitches and provide so much value and help to the industry that people flock to you for being the first business your customer comes across that actually cares about their customer and not just making money off the latest hot trend.

If you are going to start a business and you have very little competition in that space, you need to ask yourself why that is? And are there enough potential customers out there to buy your products for years to come and keep your business alive.

You need to save up and have money to start

This is very similar to what I was saying earlier, one of the biggest myths I hear coming out of so many peoples mouths is that they need to save for a few more years before they can start their business. This is so far from the truth it hurts, In the last 7 years i've experimented with many different business models and there are well over 100 businesses you could start for £0-100.

Later in this book I am going to show you how I arrange a meeting with a stranger, and within 30 minutes persuade them to pay me £1000 a month before I've even done a second's work. All you need to do is learn how to follow my proven sales system and to get yourself 2 high ticket clients who will pay you £1000 a month with 100% of it being profit right into your pocket. Unlike most businesses that try to get a 20-40% profit margin to be considered a major success. Once you get these 2 clients on board you will already be on £24,000 a year while only doing a few hours of work each day!

I promise you, you definitely do not need a lot of money to start your dream business. If you are willing to put in the time and effort, you can build a huge business without having to fork out. When I started managing my first client, I didn't even have a Wi-Fi connection at my sister's place where I was living on her sofa, homeless.

When the Times Right

Another severely limiting belief is when people believe they need to wait for the right time to start their business. Let me tell you now, there is never going to be a perfect time to start because you are always going to make mistakes because this will be a new experience for you. Your money will never be right, you may never feel better, you may never feel more motivated and most importantly you can't guarantee you will be alive long enough to make it happen in the future.

Life is very short, you cannot let your fear of failure hold you back. Everyone is afraid of failing, but that doesn't mean you should let it stop you from trying. The only way you can grow as a person is to step out of your comfort zone and force yourself to do things way before you feel like you are ready. It's hard until you get started, but once you do it's going to be even harder to stop. Start today, and if things get tough... just figure out a solution or do some research until you figure out a way around. Whatever you do though, please just start now!

You need an idea that hasn't been done before

Similar to the competition limiting belief, if you spend ages trying to come up with a brand new idea nobody has ever done before, you will give up before you have even started. There are 8 billion people in the world so trying to find someone with an original idea is like trying to find a needle in a haystack. It's going to take you forever and more importantly, what's the point? If there are business models out there already that exist and work really well already...why not just mimic that business and just add your own special twist to it that makes your business unique.

Uber wasn't a very creative idea, it was just a taxi app. But the little tweak they made to how they operate has essentially shut down half the taxi companies in the world because they cannot keep up. Imagine if the Uber owners decided to not make their app because people already had taxis, so they didn't see the point in making a taxi business. They would've missed out on billions.

Those are the top 10 myths that most new entrepreneurs including myself tend to believe when they are getting started on their journey and if you find yourself relating to any of those they will hold you back until you change that belief.

Next we are going to be focusing on what is by far the most important factor when it comes to deciding if you will succeed or fail with this book and that is YOU.

99% of wannabe entrepreneurs including myself for a very long time believe that they don't need to learn about their mindset, habits and Psychology because they assume the reason they have all these different life's problems is solely because they don't have any money.

When in reality they don't have any money because they are constantly becoming a victim to their own mind and bad habits. If there is 1 important thing to remember, it's that whatever state your mind and life are in will often reflect directly onto your business.

So if your mind is a mess, you are juggling 6 things and can't even clean your own room... There's a very strong chance that your business will also be a very sloppy and confusing mess as well. Your brain can't just turn on and off from super organised entrepreneur to depressed and unorganised when you leave your office, you must be able to balance work and life while maintaining a laser focus on your goals.

I struggled with this for years and the answer was staring me in the face for a long time but I ignored the signs, always convinced that money was what I needed to fix my personal problems. But then the money comes and you realise quickly that all your problems are still there and you have now managed to create more problems thanks to money than when you had none. No amount of money could fix the 20+ years of bad habits I had trained myself in, or stop me reaching for the easiest available dopamine rush whenever possible instead of doing what I knew I should be doing which was working my ass off to make this dream a reality instead of trying to sleep it into existence.

I spent 7 years studying everything and anything to do with business sales and marketing. Studying every single book, course and training video I could get my hands on to the point I could tell you how any business operates and makes money within a few minutes of looking at it. So why then? If I had arguably more business knowledge than most business owners... Could I not put together a functional business that lasted more than a few months!

The answer is simple really, I consistently let my personal life spill over into my work results. I would build up some good momentum for a few days and then suddenly a family argument or drama would knock my focus completely, and I would end up sitting on my phone doing nothing with my entire day knowing full well my client was expecting work completed that wasn't going to happen. I knew what the priority was, but somehow I just couldn't bring myself to do the job at hand.

Every other day I would have family and friends tell me that I should just go and get a real job and focus on a good career with some stability as my business dreams were never going to happen. I felt trapped because the thought of not working for myself was too painful to even think about long term, but my daily actions were not of someone willing to make his business work.

I would maybe do 1-2 hours each day and then just sit around pretending to do work or just study some more even though I knew everything I was being taught but just couldn't bring myself to take the action. With every bad family argument or news like my parents were sick, I would add that to the list of excuses preventing me from going all in on my dreams.

The truth was... I honestly didn't know why I wanted my dreams so badly, but then so regularly would refuse to act in a way I could move towards my dreams and progress.

But yet, even though the human mind and Psychology has always been a casual interest of mine... I never took the time to take any kind of mindset or habit training that could have helped me focus 100% and be super efficient and capable of turning things around.

Thankfully after 7 years of failures I decided to take a chance on some advanced mindset training for entrepreneurs that I was very skeptical about and within a week I already knew my life would never be the same. I took the training seriously and for the first time ever I did all the worksheets and exercises and finally understood why I was unable to build a successful business all these years.

It quickly became obvious to me that I had allowed limiting beliefs and labels to become my identity. Over the years multiple family members told me I was lazy and eventually I started to believe that I was just a naturally lazy person and so I would put in minimal effort into things because I couldn't be bothered. I was told by my family that I was a selfish person and eventually it made me into an isolated and lonely person because I believed that's who I was.

People always say that you need to be yourself and there's no point wanting to be different but this gets easily confused time and time again. We see these statements and think that we are letting people down if we start changing how we act and the things we do and focus on. We secretly or subconsciously worry that our friends and family won't like us any more if we start changing as a person.

People love consistency, so if everyone you know thinks you are shy and love you how you are... chances are you are going to be afraid of changing and becoming a confident social person because of fear for what your loved ones will think and say.

But all this is, is progression. We tend to think of our body, mind, consciousness, personality traits and society labels like race, gender etc all as the components that make us who we are. But this is completely wrong. The easiest way to explain it would be like this -

Are you familiar with computer games like GTA and Red Dead Redemption? These are games where you take control of a character in a big open world, and you get to decide what your character does each day. You choose their clothes, hairstyle, house, what they do with their time etc.

I want you to now imagine your life is just like a big open world game. Your body is the character, and your mind and the little voice inside your head that makes decisions for you is the controller.

When you play open world games you don't worry about if the clothes you wear look stupid or if someone is staring at you too often. Because you are too focused on enjoying your life in the game and focusing on completing the tasks set out in front of you.

If you have a mission that requires patience, bravery and skill you are able to dive in without any fears or doubt that your character is capable of achieving their goal. But then at the same time you are more than capable of adapting and changing your characteristics to benefit your pursuit of completing your goal.

So what I'm trying to say with this example is that if you remove all the fears of being judged, laughed at or failing and just focused on your goal like you would in a computer game. You would see that the only thing separating you from your goals is the decision to change the character you are currently playing with.

If your current character is broke, lazy, knows nothing about business, drinks 3 times a week it doesn't have to stay this way. This week I will show you how to go deep figuring out who your current character is, then we will figure out who your future desired character needs to be and what habits they need to create to become that version if you are capable of living your dreams with relative ease.

It is impossible to become a successful new version of yourself without identifying who you currently are and then planning a pathway of habits that will help you become the character capable of achieving your goals.

People who understand this, are the people who you see dominating life and it looks like everything they touch is a success. This has nothing to do with them being special or more talented than everyone else but that they understand this simple system of success.

These individuals look at the goal they want to achieve, and figure out all the action steps and habits required to go from their current situation and skill level to their desired future reality. And then once they know the steps they need to take...they do something 99% of people fail to do....they put in the effort and stick it out until the goal is achieved thanks to their daily efforts.

Your success in anything can be broken down into this formula...

A) Your current situation

B) Your goal or dream life

You now enter the steps and habits required to get from point A to B and you now have your path to success.

You may be thinking, what if I create action steps, do the steps and still fail?

That just means you calculated the steps required incorrectly and you now need to learn what you can from that experience, take the feedback and create a new and improved process to get you from your current situation to your dream life. If you don't succeed... The key is not to stop trying but to listen to your feedback and refine your action steps to something more improved. Eventually you will succeed if you continue for long enough learning from failed attempts and improving your methods and consistency.

It takes more than just hoping, wishing and thinking about something to bring it into reality. You need to move towards it with all of your energy. Mental and physical effort along with a good strategy executed daily is seriously all it takes to achieve your goals. You just need the patience and discipline to allow it to manifest into reality.

Now that we have discussed how important your mindset and actions are to the success of your business, the last thing we need to talk about in this chapter is the only thing in your business that really matters and will decide if you are successful or not.

If you do everything wrong in your business except for this one thing, there is a good chance your business will still be successful. The one secret to success is...

You have to have 1 single amazing product or service if you want to be successful and make a lot of money. This may sound obvious, but I want you to pay attention to how important having the very best service possible is.

For the first 18 months of my agency I didn't have a website, social media or any kind of marketing strategy to get new clients. What I did have was amazing service that I worked really hard to improve on each month. Each month my clients continued to pay me and even recommended me to other business owners who could benefit from my services.

You can be the best sales person in the world and sign 10 clients a week, but if your service isn't amazing you will eventually lose clients quickly and the bad reviews will start to add up to a point where nobody will ever trust you or work with you again.

Without a great service to offer clients that gets results and testimonials your business will not succeed. Do not try and offer multiple services if you haven't perfected your one main service yet.

The best selling phone of all time is the Iphone because Apple has just focused on improving the single brilliant product they have created for their customers. Instead of trying to create multiple different variations of smartphone to target to different audiences, they just keep on improving the one key product that they have already and so their customers keep coming back year after year because they know they can expect a phone they will love.

When you start your agency, do not worry about social media, building a stunning website or creating a Youtube channel. You may have been told you need those things to have a successful online business but the truth is all you need is an amazing service that your clients never want to stop paying for.

The website and all those other extra can be created in a few months time after you have started to get results for your clients. All you need to get clients to trust you is testimonials and screenshots that you can send to potential clients by email. These extra things will be helpful in the future, but they are not what is important for you to make money.

Have you ever heard of the 80/20 principle? If you haven't, go and search for it on Google once you have finished reading this book. Basically the 80/20 principle is the universal law that suggests that 80% of results come from 20% of the work you do.

This means that 80% of the jobs you will want to do in your business such as building a website and creating social media content will only give you 20% of the results in your business. When you look at your agency with the 80/20 principle in mind, you should be focusing all your efforts on the 20% of tasks that will actually bring you the best results for you and your clients. Don't waste your time doing things you can hire someone else to do in the future. Obviously there will be times where you need to do the less important tasks in your business, but just make sure that the majority of your time and energy is focused on what matters most each week.

3. THE BUSINESS MODEL

Now that you know why you should start an agency and the starting requirements, it's time for me to break down the business model so you can start to see what your first successful online business will look like when it's all put together.

By the end of this chapter you should have a good understanding of how simple it is to go from £0 making £1000s every single month from the comfort of your own home. Now I am not saying that this is going to be easy because nothing in life that is worth having is easy, and it took me 8 years to go from £0-£1000 a month before things started to take off with my marketing agency, and I started to enjoy making the type of money I could only dream of when first starting out.

In its simplest form your agency business model will look like this:

1. Find a specific type of business owner who faces a common problem and is currently making enough sales to hire someone to improve their business.
2. Find the most efficient solution to their problem that will save them time and either save or make them more money. Then package it into a service you can offer them for a monthly fee.
3. Reach out to business owners and sell them on why they need your services.

4. Get amazing results for your clients.
5. Get testimonials and case studies in order to get more clients.
6. Raise your prices.
7. Hire someone to help scale the business.
8. Add additional income streams.

If you follow these simple steps you can make a 6 figure salary within a few months from the comfort of your own home! In this book I am going to give you everything you need to get started step by step, these are the exact steps I took to go from £0 to making £4000 a month while only working a few hours a day.

1. Find a specific type of business owner who faces a common problem but is currently making enough sales to hire someone to improve their business.

This first step is where most new agency owners go wrong (Including myself). Many new agencies that haven't got much experience working with clients will try and take on any business in any industry that they can find just because they are desperate for the money. The problem with this is, if you are always working with different types of businesses you will never be able to create a consistent proven strategy to solve their problems as each business will be completely different.

You need to become the go to expert for 1 specific industry problem that 1 specific type of business owner will face. Some examples would be:

- Facebook Ads Agency for Dentists struggling to book appointments.
- Facebook Ads for online stores who have reached the limit of how far they can grow their sales.
- SMS marketing for online stores who don't understand how it works.
- Email marketing for online stores that don't have the time or knowledge to make the most profit possible from

email.
- Graphic design agency for Gyms who need to attract customers.
- Booking meetings for marketing agencies that struggle to get new clients with cold email.

You may be thinking that if you only focus on a small group of business owners it will be much harder to find someone to become your client, but the truth is it will make it so much easier!

When you create your agency based around 1 specific client type, your potential customers will be far more likely to want to work with an expert who only deals with their current problem instead of an agency that helps all kinds of business with their different problems.

Imagine if you had to have heart surgery and you had a choice of 2 doctors to perform the operation...

Doctor 1 has completed 2000 surgeries in his lifetime that included many different types of operations. These include heart surgery, hip replacements, breast reductions and even a few tumour removals. While he is undoubtedly a very talented surgeon, they have made 2 or 3 bad mistakes in their time due to how different each operation can be from his previous.

Doctor 2 on the other hand has also done 2000 surgeries in their lifetime but these have all been the same type of operation every single time. They have completed 2000 heart surgeries successfully with their results getting better and better as the years went on and they become more and more experienced with everything to do with heart operations.

Which Doctor would you want cutting you open when the time comes?

Of course you would want **Doctor 2** who has proven themselves to be the expert when it comes to fixing the exact problem we are currently facing with our heart.

The same goes for business owners looking for an agency to help their business grow, your clients want someone who focuses on their exact business model and problem everyday and has a proven strategy to get results. If you work with everybody and offer 100 services you will struggle to create proven systems to get good results consistently because every client will have needs that are very different from the last.

Later in this book I will be showing you in more detail the types of agencies you can start and the ones I recommend that are the most profitable and the easiest to get results.

If you are taking notes while reading this book I strongly advise you to make a note of this section because it is honestly so important to your success. I am only able to manage 15 clients at the same time because I have to do the same exact thing for every client so the process is easy to copy and paste time and time again. All of my clients are online stores who use Shopify and are making similar amounts of money who initially all had the same problem of not having enough time or knowledge to make the most money possible from email marketing.

I convince all of my clients to switch over to my favourite email marketing software Klaviyo and then I only need to log into my 1 account and I have instant access to all of my clients email marketing without needing to log out and switch accounts.

Because of how simple it is to replicate my work and results for clients, it makes it easier to manage many clients all at once and grow the business. Not only does it save a lot of time, it makes my life easy so I only need to work a few hours a day. Having such a simple business model makes it very straightforward for me to train workers, they can emulate my system with ease so that my business can take on more clients without me needing to work more.

2. Find the most efficient solution to their problem that will save them time and either save or make them more money. Then package it into a service you can offer them for a monthly fee.

Once you have decided on the type of business you want to work on and the problem you want to solve for them, it's time for you to create your Minimum Viable Offer.

Your MVO is the very minimum service you can provide to customers while still getting excellent results and exceeding expectations. This doesn't mean you are cutting corners and doing the bare minimum just because you don't want to do any work, it means you don't want to include any unnecessary services and features just to make your offer look good.

When you start adding lots of extra features to your service you end up wasting a lot of your time each week doing things that don't help your clients enough to make a significant difference which means you are losing out on a lot of money that could be made by spending time getting new clients.

Your clients don't care about how many features your services come with, they just want to know that they will see results when they work with you. The right MVO gets great results for clients without wasting any time on things that you do not need to focus on and your clients don't care about.

My email marketing agency has one package for all clients that offers the exact same services every single time. The price increases based on the money we are making for the client so there is no need to add extra services and features in order to make more money.

I provide the same exact service to all of my clients which is the following:

- Full management of their email marketing using Klaviyo
- Creation and optimisation of automated emails like

> abandoned carts and order confirmations
> - 3-4 Campaign emails sent out each week

That is it, that is all I promise to clients before they agree to work with me. Most people offer monthly reporting, weekly calls, Facebook advertising, social media management and all the other things they can think of because they think that is the best way to get their clients to pay them more. The truth is, the more features you add the harder it will be for you to exceed client expectations as you will be so busy juggling all these different tasks each day that you are almost certain to disappoint.

With only promising the bare minimum required for me to get them great results, it allows me the freedom to focus on one thing, that is getting them sales while only taking up the least amount of time possible and thus allowing me to find new clients and repeat the process.

Once you get to the point where you are hiring people to work for your agency you can start to implement additional services, ONLY do this if it will benefit you and your customers to do so as you now have more hands on deck to implement the services. The longer you can keep your service at the bare minimum to keep your customers happy the better, don't give yourself extra work for no reason if you have a service that gets results already.

3. Reach out to business owners and sell them on why they need your services.

Once you have decided on the service you want to offer your clients it's now time for you to choose your pricing (which we will discuss later in the book) and then start approaching potential clients and selling them on your services.

When you are just starting out, you will want to either work for a cheap monthly rate or offer a few free trials so that you can start getting results and testimonials for your business, this will make it a lot easier to get big paying clients in the future once you can prove you are the expert for their niche.

The most effective way to get clients will be cold email and referrals, later in this book we will discuss the following:

- How to find potential clients and their contact information.
- How I create emails that people will actually reply to.
- How to get someone to agree to a phone call with you.
- My simple strategy to convert 90% of people over the phone.
- How to get paid before you have done any work.
- How to get referrals.

4. Get amazing results for your clients

Whatever service you choose to offer will come with learning/ studying that you will have to get over in order to be successful. Whether you decide to do Facebook marketing, SMS Marketing or Email marketing you will need to go and find learning materials for your chosen service. Unfortunately, I cannot teach you how to get results in this book because each service could have it's own 200 pages book just for beginners.

What I will do though is show you where you can go and learn the skills required to fully understand the bare minimum needed in order to get great results for your clients. I will also give you an idea of what great results look like for various agency types and for your clients.

You will have to do some serious studying in the first few weeks of your business if you are serious about being successful. You should be searching for courses and youtube videos that show you step by step how to get results doing the service you want to offer to your clients.

You don't have to become a master of your service within a few weeks, but you do need to learn enough about your business that you can do the basics well and then start to improve on the job as nothing beats experience. You also need to be able to confidently answer any questions and objections your potential clients might have when you are trying to sell yourself to them, if you are not always learning and improving your business will fail before it even starts!

5. Get testimonials and case studies to get more clients

Once you have started to get great results for your clients it's time for you to start asking for testimonials, referrals and to start creating case studies that show future clients how you manage to get results for your current clients.

The more evidence you have of your results and the more client testimonials you get the easier the sale will become each time. Anyone can claim to be an expert but when your potential customers can see that businesses just like theirs have worked with you and saw results so good they were willing to vouch for your services, they will instantly trust you a lot more!

Later in this book I will show you when the right time to ask for a testimonial is as well as the best kind of testimonials and reviews you can ask for that will help you to get the most sales.

6. Raise your prices

Once you start to work with multiple clients and your agency is getting consistent results for your clients you will want to start to raise your prices as you will most likely be undercharging for your services.

When I first started my agency my pricing was painfully low for the value I was bringing to my clients, I was making £70,000 a month for 1 client while only getting paid £500 a month which is less than 1%. On average I was only charging 1% of the sales I was making for clients as my fee.

Once I reached 14 clients varying in monthly fees from £100 - £1000 I quickly realised I needed to stop working with the small clients who couldn't afford to pay more and focus on my bigger clients who I was making £20,000+ a month for and who I could ask to increase my fee from 1% to 3% per month.

3% doesn't sound like a lot but that means my monthly income would instantly triple while having to do less work than before as I got rid of my small clients who were costing me money in wasted time.

This took me from someone barely getting by each month to making more money each month than I could of ever dreamed of and the crazy thing is there was still room to increase my prices in the future.

Once you have completed this step and begin to hire people to help your business scale further, you will be able to improve the quality of your services and then once again increase your prices from 3% to 5% and even 10% a month.

At this point you will be making at least £10-20k a month even after you pay your staff and will be in the position to work with monster clients who will be able to pay you £5/10/20k a month on their own each month.

7. Hire someone to help scale the business

You are only human so there's only so much work you can handle each day. Eventually you will reach a point where the only way your business can grow further is if you hire someone to do some of the work for you.

Whether you need someone to focus on getting results for your clients or even someone who will go out and book you meetings with potential clients, hiring someone will eventually become a must in order to grow your business to the next level.

Later in this book I will show you the best places to find reliable workers for your agency and I will also show you how I train and choose my staff when I am hiring someone to come onto my team.

8. Add additional income streams

Once you have mastered your agency and are bringing in a lot of money each month after perfecting your business to run smoothly and efficiently you will want to look to use your business model to create new income streams. These include things such as:

- Online courses
- Ebooks
- Guides
- 1 on 1 consulting
- Group consulting
- Affiliate marketing
- Membership sites

These are all brilliant ways to take your business models and systems and turn them into products that people can use to grow their own businesses without you needing to do any additional work once they are created.

Once you write the script for an ebook, you can then use the same script to create an audio book and even an online course. Take all the content and systems you have and recycle them into different types of content as your customers will all enjoy consuming content in their own particular way.

With the power of your previous results and testimonials you should be able to sell your content online without many issues at all, as you will be living the perfect laptop lifestyle that millions of people dream of.

You have now seen the entire business model of your new agency, these simple steps are all you need to follow in order to become a successful business owner in the next few months.

This framework will be very similar and successful no matter what agency type you decide to start. We will now be moving onto the next the chapter in this book which will help you to decide what type of agency you would like to create.

4. YOUR AGENCY SERVICE

Each different agency or consultancy service could have multiple books written on them before you begin to get a good understanding of how to be really good at delivering your service, so I won't be teaching you Facebook Ads, Email Marketing or anything like that in this book. What I will do is break down what will be expected from you and also show you the best places to learn the basic skills required to deliver your services with confidence within the next few weeks.

If you already know what service you want to provide then feel free to just skip to that section in this chapter, if you are undecided on which service and what niche you want to work in then this chapter will hopefully help you to make a decision.

So below are my top suggestions for services you can study and learn the required basic fundamental skills to start your business in the next few weeks:

Advertising Agency

Advertising agencies are probably the most profitable agency you can start if you are able to get your head around the various advertising platforms that are available to business owners currently.

Some Facebook advertising agencies I know charge up to 20% of their clients monthly ad spend as their monthly fee. 20% might not sound like a huge number but if you are managing the advertising for an online store who spend £50,000 a month on advertising you would be looking at a whopping £10,000 a month going straight into your pocket!

Even if they were only making £10,000 a month that is still £2000 a month for you to manage just 1 client which is a bigger wage than any full time job I ever worked.

If you plan on starting an advertising agency I would strongly recommend you focus on mastering 1 platform at a time as if you focus on learning more than 1 at a time your skills on each platform will take far longer to develop.

The most popular advertising platforms out there include most of the social medias such as:

- Facebook Advertising
- Instagram Advertising
- Google Advertising
- Snapchat Advertising
- Twitter Advertising
- Youtube Advertising

These places are great advertising platforms for online businesses because they all have a lot of users who tell the platform what they like and dislike based on the things we look at and interact with on social media. These companies are always trying to think of new data they can learn about us so that advertisers can continue to get results and keep paying.

I would recommend starting with Facebook/Instagram advertising as they have proven to be the number 1 advertising platform for many brands in the last 5 years. Other platforms have started to get more competitive which is why you should look into other Advertising softwares in the future but for now Facebook Advertising should be your choice.

The reason why advertising agencies are so great is because almost every business needs to be running paid adverts if they want to grow their business, the funny thing is, most business owners suck at advertising.

They are passionate about whatever product or service they provide whether that be an online clothing brand owner obsessed with creating beautiful designs or a dentist focused on making sure they are the best dentist they can be. There is not enough time in the week for them to focus on providing an amazing product or service as well as crafting out detailed advertising campaigns and monitoring all the tests and variations involved in creating winning adverts.

This is where you can step in and be the hero their business needs to succeed by offering them your advertising services which will make them money as well as save them time so they can focus on other areas of the business they care about.

You can find free and affordable training videos that with teach you all the information you will need to get started delivering a good standard of results in the following places:

- Youtube
- Udemy
- Amazon

There is more than enough free content on Youtube that focuses on Facebook advertising for local businesses and ecommerce stores. If you spend a few hours each day for the next 2-3 weeks studying and taking notes on everything you can find to do with Facebook advertising, you will have more than enough knowledge needed to approach clients and get results.

Marketing Agency

Similar to an advertising agency in the sense that the goal of your marketing agency will be to make sales and help to grow your clients business. The main difference here being Advertising is something you have to keep increasing your investment if you want sales for your business to increase as you will typically pay per click or view of your advert whereas Marketing is often more focused on organic sales without needing to keep investing money such as Email Marketing, Seo Marketing and Social Media Marketing.

All of these agency types work but can take a few weeks to months before you start seeing results for clients. Typically your clients will be understanding of the time it takes to see results as long as you are clear about it when you are selling them on your services.

Of the 3 services named I would of course suggest that you start your own email marketing agency as this is the service I offer for my clients because it suits who I am perfectly. I work with on-line retail stores but there are many different businesses out there that need an expert to send sales emails to their customers.

The thing that separates email marketing from all the other forms of advertising and marketing is that your email list is the only thing you have 100% control over. If you use Facebook Advertising or Google you have to follow their guidelines and rules or else your account will get suspended and then you won't be able to deliver your service to your clients.

At the time of writing this at least half of my clients have had their advertising accounts temporarily suspended during the most important time of the year, between Black Friday and Christmas.

With email marketing once someone has opted into your email list you now have legal permission to email them and sell them your products whenever you want and however you want. If you send something risky you may get a few people unsubscribe and stop you sending them emails anymore but the likelihood is you wouldn't get your email banned. Even if your email address was blacklisted for some reason, as long as you have access to your list of subscribers you can always get a new email and continue to contact the list.

Email has been around for as long as the internet has existed and even though people like to say "Email is dead" the truth is email will probably outlast every social media and advertising platform that exists today. Everybody needs an email address to do anything online in the modern era, whether you are signing into Facebook or buying a product. You need an email address and so does everybody else in the world that has an internet connection.

Facebook is always being taken to court and sued for privacy breaches and other violations so there is no doubt that email would most definitely survive longer than Facebook or any other website that exists today. So if you want to master a skill that you will be able to use for your entire lifetime without having to worry about the site closing down or you getting banned... Email marketing is the way to go.

As the role of an email marketing agency requires less work and generates less money for companies than advertising, you typically can charge up to 10% of what you earn your clients each month through email. You will often find that 90% of businesses making under £200k a month haven't got a focused email marketing strategy that is designed to make the most sales possible, so they are leaving a lot of money on the table and will be very grateful and happy to pay you for something they never could imagine would be so profitable for their business.

To begin learning a marketing agency skill such as email marketing you can start by going to Youtube, Udemy or from books that talk specifically about the agency skill you want to learn.

Lead Generation Agency

There is a huge demand for agencies who know how to generate warm leads (potential customers) for businesses. If you can master the cold email process from start to finish you can charge other agencies and business owners a lot of money each month to bring them in new customers.

If you are a lead generation agency for marketing agencies their average client will pay them around £1000 - £5000 a month and if you are capable of getting them 3 clients a month you can easily charge up to £5000 a month for your services since they will be making far more than that in return.

I have seen many people become very successful from their lead generation agencies because so many businesses have no clue when it comes to cold sales and waste a lot of time and money trying different strategies that barely get any results. If you can spend 2 days studying everything you can find online to do with succeeding with cold email, you will have more than enough knowledge on how to make sure your emails go straight into inboxes and not spam folders, as well as how to create emails that people open and want to reply to which is all you need to know to make your lead generation agency a success.

Once you have created your cold email framework you can test it works by trying to get yourself clients with your email strategy. If you use the framework I give you in this book that will be an excellent place to start if you combine it with good email practises such as using a paid email and getting all the right verifications set up.

Always be testing and improving your sales process and make sure you stick to one niche industry so you can create a system that works consistently without having to be changed and edited depending on what industry you are selling to.

Website Agency

Many years ago you would have needed to know how to code and build websites from scratch if you wanted to start your own website agency. Nowadays the majority of businesses use a simple easy to use website host such as Shopify where anybody can figure out how to create their website within a few hours.

Just because anyone can build a website today, doesn't mean that many people are very good at it. Typically business owners will do a terrible job of their website before they get an expert to help them. A website's conversion rate is incredibly important to the success of a business each year and so the ability to optimise websites to get more sales is an incredibly valuable skill that can bring you a lot of money.

If a website's current conversion rate is 1.2% which means for every 100 visitors the average amount of people actually purchasing is just slightly more than 1 the chances are you could dramatically increase this percentage. Imagine this business currently makes £500,000 a year and you step in and get their website conversions up from 1.2% to 2.4% this would instantly double their yearly revenue and get them an extra £500,000 a year. With a few strategic changes to their website like increasing speed, cleaning up the look and adding buttons in the right places you could charge a massive fee to your clients for the initial changes and then get paid monthly for maintenance.

Video/Photo Agency

Almost all businesses can benefit from high quality video and image content in one way or another, people engage better with videos and images than they do with text so most business owners understand that high visuals are a must for their brand image.

If you or someone you know is great with a camera and editing there are endless opportunities for you to make a lot of money. Anyone can buy a good camera, but it takes practise and a lot of effort to turn a normal photo or video into a stunning visual that engages an audience.

Choose a niche that will require your services on a regular basis and are already generating a lot of money such as online clothing stores who always need images and videos to showcase their products. If you know how to make their designs look amazing and help them get more sales you can charge more money per shoot than a lot of photographers make in a month.

Graphic Design Agency

Similar to a photo/video agency a graphic design agency is something that the majority of online businesses can benefit from in many ways. Whether you are creating graphics for Facebook ads, social media posts or emails there are many different ways that business owners could benefit from a high quality graphic designer who can create stunning branded content on a regular basis.

Once again I think successful online stores would be the best people to target here as they will be able to afford to pay a decent rate because your graphics will help them make more sales and maintain brand consistency.

Photoshop is the most famous software that graphic designers use but I would recommend using Canva if you are just getting started as it is free to use and is the software I have used for all my graphics in the last 2 years. Canva is incredibly easy to use and will have you feeling like a professional graphic designer within a few hours.

Specialised Niche Agencies

If the above suggestions didn't sound like a good fit for you, this is your opportunity to get creative and follow something more suited to your passions and interests.

There are a few TV shows in the UK and US that are based around dating agencies that specialise in finding celebrities and millionaires potential life partners to take out on dates and hopefully help them find love.

These successful people typically have busy lives and struggle to find time to date, when they do date they will often worry that the person they are dating is only using them for their money. This can cause them to have a major pain point in their lives that they wish they could fix.

If you know there is a group of people who all share the same problem and you know how to provide them with the bridge to take them from their current situation, to their desired situation. You can package that up into a service and get these people to pay you in exchange for results.

5. DEFINING YOUR NICHE

A common mistake new agency owners make (including myself) is that they are afraid to narrow down their customers to 1 specific business type and instead try to be an agency that works with all kinds of business types in the hopes of getting any client they can find.

If you try to work with multiple niches at once you will always be having to learn what works best for each business and will never be able to create a proven and tested strategy to get clients results quickly which will allow you to get testimonials and then sign new clients easily.

Nobody wants to work with a marketing agency that is willing to work with everyone and anyone because you won't be proven at getting results for their specific business type and therefore they will look to find someone who is an expert in the niche.

When I first started my agency my first few clients were a Chip shop, a Garden Office/Shed building company, an opticians and an online clothing store. None of these businesses had anything to do with each other and so with each client I began working with I was starting from nothing and had to figure out what worked and what didn't.

This meant that I spent most of my time offering random services to different clients with no real strategy or direction because I was juggling so many different things at once that none of my work was high quality.

Across these brands I was offering the following services at once:

- Facebook advertising
- Facebook posts
- Instagram posts
- Photography/Videos
- Lead generation
- Email marketing
- Web design
- Chat Bots

I truly believed that the more services I offered the more clients would want to work with me and this is what it took to create a successful online marketing agency. The reality was, trying to do all these things at once meant I was unable to become good at any of the services I offered because I never had time to focus on 1 particular thing consistently.

Not only was every single service I offered poor quality but I also was unable to tell people what my business was because I had no idea myself. The truth was I was just pretending to be a marketing agency hoping that I would work things out as I went along.

It wasn't until I decided to focus 100% on email marketing for online clothing brands that I was finally able to start improving my skills and mastering my service. I went from juggling 50 things each day to only having to log into the same email software each day and following almost the exact same strategy with each client to get them consistent results each day.

I am now able to test what works and what doesn't each and every day so that my service is always getting better and things are more efficient with every new client that comes on board.

When my potential clients land on my social media pages they no longer see a boring and generic bio saying things that they don't care about such as *Entrepreneur Marketing Agency Owner For Busi-*

nesses and they now see something like *I Help Shopify Stores Increase Their Sales By Up To 40% Each Month.*

Do you see how powerful choosing your niche can be? The first bio doesn't catch the attention of anybody because nobody can relate to it. There's so many experts out there who specialise in what your potential clients want that they are just going to ignore your business and focus on finding an agency that actually works with people like them on a daily basis.

Be specific with who you are targeting and want to work with, you need to be clear on who you serve and how you serve them and then do not compromise. You should be able to sell your services to potential customers in just 1 sentence, if you cannot do that you are not clear on what your service is yet. You need to be able to sell in just 1 sentence because that is all your potential customers will get to read in your social media bios.

My Facebook, Instagram and Linkedin all say

"I currently help Shopify stores earning at least £10,000 a month increase their sales by up to 40% with email marketing"

This is such a powerful tool to have in your belt, the easier it is to understand what your business is and the results you offer the more sales you will make. No business owner cares what features your service has or what my credentials are, they want to know if I can get results for businesses just like theirs.

Before I decided on my niche and I was trying to work with anyone I could find, I would have to do hours of research and preparation before a sales meeting with a potential client because I had no knowledge on their business model, what the owner was struggling with or how to get results in this industry.

I would create a huge 40 page presentation filled with all the features and benefits I could think of to convince them to let me try and get them new customers. Every time I would just look stupid and nervous as I tried to freestyle my way through these meetings pretending I had a clue about what I was saying.

Nowadays my last 17 clients have all been pretty much the same process from start to finish because they are all the same niche. With every client the process gets easier and easier and the results keep on getting better. Long gone are the days of hours of research and preparation before doing the long journey to meet up with the potential client only to nervously fail and waste my time.

Now I simply send over a cold email and wait to see if they are interested in a phone call. Once I am on the phone call I ask them why they agreed to speak to me and if it is clear that I could help them make more sales and give them what they are looking for, I will promise them amazing results with confidence because I know I have done it for 17 brands just like them already.

With every client you take on you will be seen as a bigger expert in your industry. This will allow you to charge more money because you provide a specialised service instead of a service for everyone and anyone. Sales has become so simple for me now that I am considered an expert that I honestly have never seen what half of my clients even look like and I have only met 1 or 2 in person.

These clients are still incredibly happy to recommend me to other business owners and pay month after month because I am so consistent with my process and results. This can only come when you get really specific with who you want your clients to be so you can build amazing systems to get them results time and time again.

The more specific the easier it will be for you to get clients and results, instead of offering Facebook advertising for all local businesses you should be more specific and be the expert for dentists, restaurants or gyms. If you were offering lead generation for all businesses, narrow that down to lead generation for marketing agencies and then you can narrow it even further to just email marketing agencies and then maybe one day I will hire you myself.

You only need 2 clients to earn a good full time wage so please do not ignore this chapter and pursue multiple niches. I understand you may not know what the best niche to choose is just yet, but just try and stick to 1 for a few weeks or months before changing to another niche if you are unhappy. I had no idea what niche I wanted to choose but I just kept on trying everything I could think of until I did email for shopify stores for a few months and realised that was the right niche for me.

Being efficient in business will save you a lot of time and make you a lot of money and the only way to be efficient is to make sure your business knows its niche and can sell it's services in just one sentence.

6. CRAFTING YOUR BRAND MESSAGE

Once you know exactly what niche you want to target it's time for you to begin to understand who your perfect customer is. If you don't have a detailed understanding of your customer and how they think you will struggle to make any sales. The secret to sales is being able to convince someone you can take them from their current situation that they want to get out of and provide them with the solution to live in their desired life situation.

This could be a busy online store owner who wishes they didn't have to work 60 hours a week because half of their time is spent doing jobs they don't understand so they are losing money. In this case, their current situation or "pain point" is that they are doing everything in their business, including the jobs they suck at and their desired situation is that they wish they could work less hours and make more money.

This is a brief description of the customer avatar that I use when selling to my potential clients. Your business needs to create its own customer avatar in order to completely understand how your customer thinks and how to make them truly believe that your service is what they need to go from their current painful situation to their desired situation.

Now that I understand who my customer avatar is, it is easy for me to sell to them because I already know what their problem is and I have a proven solution for them to benefit from.

My solution for busy ecommerce store owners who want to work less and earn more is that I manage their entire email marketing strategy, which instantly opens up multiple hours my clients would of had to spend on it each week while also making them 4-5X more money from email than they could of managed themselves without my proven strategies.

You need to make it your obsession to know everything about your target customer and how they think, the easiest way I find to do this is by completing a customer avatar worksheet that will force you to learn who your customer is inside and out.

The more information you can collect on your target customer, the easier it will be to sell your services to them as you will know what they want and what problems they might object to.

I will end this chapter by leaving you with the customer avatar worksheet questions I use in my business. Do your research and answer these questions to the best of your ability and this will help you get sales much faster than having to guess what your customers are want from you.

Here are the worksheet questions, stop reading this book for a moment and take the time to answer questions these now:

1. What keeps your customer awake at night?

2. What are they afraid of?

3.What makes them angry?

4.What makes them happy?

5. What is their biggest frustration?

6. What trends are going to affect them?

7. What is their secret desire, one they wouldn't even tell their therapist?

8. Do they have any built-in beliefs?

9. Do they talk a certain way?

10. What social media platforms do they use?

11. What books have they read?

12. What does their day look like?

13. What is the most common problem they are like to have?

14. What is the one thing they'd crave above anything else?

15. Would I pay for this service if you were them? Or read this blog? Or pre-order this book?

7. HOW TO GET CLIENTS

Getting your first few clients will probably be the hardest thing you have to do when you start your agency. This isn't because your service will be hard to sell or your client does not need your services, but because you will naturally be nervous and inexperienced with selling your services and will most likely suffer from Imposter Syndrome.

*Imposter syndrome can be defined as a collection of feelings of inadequacy that persist despite evident success. '***Imposters***' suffer from chronic self-doubt and a sense of intellectual fraudulence that override any feelings of success or external proof of their competence.* (hbr.org)

For the first 6 months that you are in business you will most likely feel like a fraud that doesn't really know what you are doing. This isn't because you actually are frauding your clients, but your mind will take a while to adjust and accept that you are really a marketing agency owner who works from home. As long as you focus on improving your skills each day and your service provides clear value to customers, you will be seen as an expert in your industry.

If you are brand new and lacking in experience just take the time to be honest with your potential clients and let them know you are giving them a huge discount on your service because you need to build your portfolio and testimonials up. If you pretend to be this experienced marketing master that has already made millions, you will have a hard time living up to customer expectations.

The more experience you get in providing your service and getting results, the more confident you will slowly become in selling your services to new clients. Everyday that you spend working on your skills and getting results for your clients, whether they are paying or free trials, you will gain valuable experience that will increase your confidence when it comes to selling your services.

Not only will you start to get more confident in selling your services but the more experience you gain the better understanding you will have about how valuable you are to your clients. If you know you are worth £10,000 a month on average to a client, why not charge £500 a month or even £1000 a month? Your fee would only be 5-10% of the sales you generate each month which is a very fair deal for both sides.

Sales can be a very stressful process if you let it be, but with the right systems and beliefs in place it can be the most exciting part of your business. I used to be terrified of selling my services as I had no clear strategy in place that I knew would get results and I doubted my skills as an email marketer for a long time before things came together.

After trying every possible sales method I could find over the last few years, I now have a proven sales process that any agency owner can use to get sales in their business. This system took me from 3 clients to 14 in just 3 months and to be completely honest I only spent a few hours on this each month before hiring someone to do my sales for me.

If you follow this framework that I am going to give you in the rest of this chapter, you will definitely get sales. You may not get sales straight away as you may need to change some things to make it work for you and your agency but if you are consistent you will definitely get a client with some patience.

So here is my proven sales system that has allowed me to scale my business 5X in the last year:

1. Finding Potential Clients
2. Contacting The Owner
3. Arranging A Phone Call
4. Selling On The Phone
5. Onboarding

1. Finding Potential Clients

There are many different ways available for you to find potential business clients to work with. I currently use the following methods:

Find the social media platform your niche uses the most.

Every niche has a social media platform where you can always expect to find them, more often than not that platform is Instagram. I work with online clothing brands that rely on beautiful visuals to sell their products so Instagrams visual focused platform is the perfect place for them to promote their business.

Depending on your niche it will be your job to find out where your potential clients are most likely to spend their time. Your niche may be on Instagram, Facebook, Linkedin or Twitter. Once you know the best place to find potential clients you will want to start following them so you can keep track of their business without having to find them again.

Purchase a lead list

This method will save you a lot of time but may be seen as an expensive purchase when you are just getting started. If you are servicing an ecommerce site like I am you can go to a website like **Builtwith** and then quickly search for business owners that meet your niche requirements and download a list of thousands of your perfect potential customers within minutes.

Other great sites include:

Hunter.io (Find leads and also find the company emails to contact)
D7 Leadfinder (Great for finding local businesses)
Fiverr (Hire someone to find leads for you at reasonable prices)

If your niche is local businesses and not e-commerce you should be able to download your leads a lot cheaper as they are typically easier to find as they have a physical store unlike online stores that can be registered anywhere in the world.

Contacting The Owner

Once you have found a way to find potential customers it's time to start doing your research to see if they would be a good fit for your agency and also you want to find the owner so you can contact them personally.

When I first started trying to get clients I would send out the exact same copy and pasted email to hundreds of brands with a very poor to non existent success rate. Out of roughly 1000 emails sent out I probably got 10 responses which is not a great response rate for the time it took me to send each email.

If your leads think your email message is simply copy and pasted like 99% of the agency emails they receive, they will ignore it and stop reading within 5 seconds. The secret to getting responses from your cold emails is to make sure the first line of your email is personalised to be specifically about the business owner or business.

When you include a personalised first line in your emails your leads will instantly be more likely to feel connected to you and be willing to read the rest of what you have to say in the email.

Some good first line examples would be:

"Hey Steve, I just wanted to wish you a late happy birthday for 2 days ago... I can't believe your wife bought you a ps5 im so jealous!"

"Hey Jessica, congratulations on recently winning your local business of the year award! You and your team definitely deserved to win"

"Hey Dave, your latest collection of hoodies has to be my favourite launch I have seen all year. The stitching style you included is stunning, I can tell you really care about your products!"

You can find the Information required to create an awesome first line by either searching the business on Linkedin and then find the owner, or by searching the business on the companies house directory and then finding the owner under the director position.

Once you have found the owner you want to search for them on Instagram, Facebook or even Google search their name. Your goal is to find out something personal about them that will show them you have done your research and haven't just copy and pasted a generic message.

Finding a personal thing to say about each client may sound like it's very time consuming but I promise you the increase in replies and sales will make it worth it very quickly. When I first started using personal lines in my emails it only took me 5 emails before I signed a client for £500 a month.

Arranging A Phone Call

After your personal line you now want to introduce yourself and your business with as much social proof as possible with a short 1 sentence case study.

The point of this 1 sentence case study is to quickly show your lead that you have experience getting results for their niche and could also get the same results for their business.

It is important you include this case study as your leads are only going to be interested in your services if you can quickly show that you get results for businesses just like their business. Some examples would be:

I recently helped Little Pepe's, an Italian restaurant just like yours go from £5000 a week in sales to £9000 a week in sales using Facebook Ads

I recently helped Dark Apparel, an online clothing brand similar to your business go from earning £3000 a month from email marketing to £15000 a month using my proven email strategies on Klaviyo

I just finished helping Ocean Agency, a marketing agency just like yours bring in 5 new clients a month for the last 4 months using my expert cold email strategies.

If you currently don't have any experience or case studies, you will want to focus on letting them know that you are offering a service that will save them a lot time and increase their money. If they ask for proof of your work, be honest and tell them you are new but are confident in getting results for them. If they are still hesitant, you can always offer them a brief trial to prove yourself in exchange for a testimonal.

Now you have started your email with a personal line, then followed it up by showing you can take them from their current situation to a much better situation if they work with you. The last thing to do is let them know you have seen some things in their business you think you could improve and then ask them if they have time for a phone call either this week or next week.

Telling them that you have already looked at their business and have spotted some areas to improve is the final ingredient that will make your leads want to respond to you. Now they feel like an expert has looked at their business and noticed some problems that are costing them money, they would be crazy to ignore what you have to say.

Some examples would be:

I have been signed up to your email list for a few weeks and have noticed some instant changes I would like to make that would increase your monthly sales straight away. Do you have time for a call this week or next?

I couldn't help but notice you are paying for newspaper advertising when your business would get more customers for cheaper using more effective advertising methods, do you have time for a quick call?

I was recently on your website and noticed some very outdated graphics that are putting your customers off from buying from you, do you have time for a call this week and we can discuss how to make your site more in line with your brand message?

When you put it all together your emails should look like this:

Hey **(Lead Name), (Personalised Line)**

My name is Robert and **(Short case study)**

I couldn't help but notice **(Politely tell them their business needs help)**

Do you have time for a call this week?

This is the exact cold email strategy I currently use for my business and gets leads to arrange a sales call with me. Follow this framework and use it with your agency and you should start to see results quickly!

Selling On The Phone

For years I was scared of selling on the phone, the thought of having to think of smart sales related things to say that would convince leads to become my client felt terrifying.

How embarrassing would it be if they asked me a question on the phone that I didn't know the answers to? At the time I thought this would be the end of the world and so I steered clear of the phone for as long as I could. The thought of cold calling a business owner and knowing the right things to say so they didn't tell me to go away and never call again made me want to throw up in fear!

To be fair to the old version of myself, I still hate the idea of cold calling an random business owner who has never heard of me and it's something I personally would never do.

Warm calls on the other hand are a lot less scary and a lot easier to get a successful outcome from.

Cold Calls - Nobody likes to answer the phone to random numbers, especially if it is because they are being sold something. Even if your service is the best in the world, most people won't appreciate you calling them without permission and won't even pay attention to what you have to offer.

Warm Calls - Once you have already contacted the business owner through email and they have expressed an interest in your services and handed their phone number to you, you now have a huge opportunity to secure yourself a new client. Once I have a phone call scheduled with a lead I am always confident that using my warm call strategy will get me 9/10 leads to convert into clients.

Once you are on the phone with a warm lead all you have to do is follow my simple 2 question strategy that I use on all of my phone calls to get my leads to tell me everything I need to know to persuade them to start working with me.

These amazing questions that have helped me sign my 17 clients to date will look simple, but the power behind these 2 questions will completely change your life.

My super money making phone call questions are:

-       Why did you jump on this phone call today, can you tell me a little about your business?
-       What made you want to talk to me specifically?

These 2 simple questions should be asked at the very beginning of your call after the initial introductions and should give you enough information for you to close the sale. If you can find out exactly why your lead is looking for help, the current state of their business and what their goals are, you can then promise them things they actually care about instead of offering them a bunch of things they never even wanted.

Let's imagine I spoke to a clothing brand owner for my email marketing agency and before asking them any questions about what they are looking for I just started talking about all the different features my service offers hoping that one of the features would get them to agree to buy.

If you don't know what your leads want, you are just going to offer them a bunch of random features that they probably don't even care about, or understand how they can even help their business grow.

The 2 things business owners care about is usually "How much money will I make or save" and "Will it save me time each week". The only way you will be able to find out what your lead prioritises is simply by asking them.

Once you know what it is that they want and are looking for from you, if you are still confident you can help them all you have to do is repeat back to them that you can definitely help them reach their goals.

After you have convinced them that you are the right person to help them get the results they are looking for, you will want to tell them your price. Typically I like to compare the fee to how much I will be making the client each month, so that way the offer is too good to refuse. This will look something like this on the call:

On average when I work with a client of your size I generate them at least £20,000 a month so my fee will be £2000 a month.

Typically we generate at least 10 new leads for clients every month which means you should convert £10,000 a month in extra business so my fee will is £1000 a month.

Once you have told them the fee you want to charge, stay silent and wait for their response before speaking again. Give them time to process the information and see that your fee is actually worth the money. If you start nervously rambling on after you say your price this will make you look weak and unconfident.

If they object or want a lower price, you just need to assure them that with agencies you get what you pay for. A premium fee comes with premium results and you will be invoicing them once a month so they can stop the service at anytime without being tied into a contract.

Onboarding

Once they have agreed to work with you, you will want to email them over a list of things they will need to do for you to get started, such as give you admin access to their ad accounts and access to their image folders. On this list of things they need to do, you will also want to ask them for their business address details to put on the invoice you are planning on sending over later that day.

Then you will want to create an invoice using a simple template that can be found with a Google search. I have a template in my Google sheets that I use when creating invoices for my clients.

Let your new client know that as soon as the invoice is paid you will get started and they will usually pay the invoice on the same day.

Congratulations, you just got a new client to pay you!Remember the date you invoiced them and then send them an invoice on the same date every month moving forward.

Referrals

The easiest way to get someone to want to work with you is if someone they trust has reffered you to them. My 2nd and 3rd clients came after my first client was so pleased with my work, that he told his friends to start working with me.

Because they already trusted my client, all I had to do was have a quick 5 minute phone call with them and they had already agreed to pay me whatever I wanted to ask for.

Do amazing work for your clients and then once they have made it clear to you that they love you work, ask them if they know anyone else who might be able to benefit from your services and they will be happy to help you out. You can also offer discounts on your services in exchange for a refferal if you need a bigger incentive.

8. PRICING

I have mentioned earlier in this book about why you need to move away from the mindset of being paid by the hour, if you want to be successful you need to charge based on your value and not your time. If you were to charge £20 an hour for your services you would need to work a soul destroying 62 hours a week to make £5000 a month.

Even though working for yourself is more rewarding than working for another company, if you are being forced to work 62 hours a week just to make £60,000 a year you won't be very happy with your life, I can promise you that.

You need to charge your clients a fair price based on the value you will bring to your customers. If you will be managing your clients Facebook ads and you generate them £20,000 in sales a month, you could charge up to £2000 a month in fees which is only 10% when you did all the work is a fair deal for anyone.

I completely understand that if you are just starting out you will be scared of charging clients a lot of money when you haven't got the confidence or evidence of results yet. If this is the case, you can always offer new clients a short term free trial in exchange for a testimonial and an agreement for them to become a paying customer in the future.

I personally hated the idea of free trials when I was starting out, so I just charged a low amount to clients that I knew would make it easy for me to exceed expectations quickly. After a few months of great results you can show your clients your results compared to the tiny fee you are charging and ask for more money.

When I first started my agency I thought I needed to be competitive with the lowest priced social media services on the market. Especially because I was inexperienced and more importantly unconfident in my own abilities. So I would charge between £100 and £300 a month for full management services, advertising spend and even photography!

But when you think about it, after taxes and costs and time invested.... I realised even if i had 20 clients I would be broke and also would require more than 24 hours in a day to get the work done for all these clients.

Once I started to feel confident in my abilities and I had increased my knowledge on email marketing through experience and online courses from the best minds in business, I knew I needed to increase my prices if I wanted this business to change my life. I saw hundreds of marketing agency gurus on Youtube making £2000+ a month from their clients and I just couldn't figure out how they could justify asking for such a large fee when they were fairly new in starting their business.

I tried raising my prices to between £500 and £1000 a month and immediately all my family and friends told me that seemed like far too much to be asking for. And that I should reduce the costs to a cheaper rate so I could definitely secure the sale and live off the little fee which would be better than no money at all because I aimed too high and got rejected.

Stubborn as always I continued with my higher pricing and was met with a lot of resistance from the businesses I was pitching to. Mainly because I was asking for this money without much evidence or clear process as to why so much money was required for some social media posts.

As I always do when I have an issue that needs fixing, I began to do my research on how the best businesses price their products and services. After months of research and learning from various experts here is what I discovered.

The cheaper I priced my service, the lower quality customer I would attract.

This isn't to say there was anything wrong with the customer, it just means they were less of a good fit for a successful marketing agency for the following reasons:

1. Because they can only afford a low fee, the money is highly important to them and they will demand a lot from you in exchange for a low pay rate and not a lot of help. They will also have the most issues for you to deal with and payment disputes.

2. The more expensive and premium your service is, the higher quality customers you will attract as they can afford your service and are looking for an expert they can just leave to get on with the work and only check in now and again for updates and changes.

3. The more expensive your service or product, the more seriously your customers will take your business and time. Sometimes charging a small fee will leave people thinking your service isn't good enough for their needs and they will go and seek a more expensive option offering the exact same thing. That's why 90% of books never get finished because paying under £10 isn't a big enough commitment on your part to feel like you have to finish it and follow the steps inside.

Believe it or not, you are doing your customers a disservice if you don't charge premium rates. I wasn't able to give my first clients the service they wanted because I was too scared to ask for the money and ad spend required to make that happen. When I started charging more I was able to easily get better results while automating the process and making more money for less effort.

So increase your prices to a point you feel uncomfortable asking for, make your customers feel proud to own your product instead of thinking they just got something cheap that will do for now. Make them excited to use your service instead of wondering if it's actually going to work.

Go and look what the premium rates are in your industry and then find out what they offer which makes them different to you. The likelihood is that they have just positioned themselves to a small specific niche of people who are looking for something that really expresses who they are or what they do.

You don't have to charge the same prices as the best agencies in your niche straight away but make sure you are charging a fair price to yourself compared to what they are charging. Don't fall into the trap that a lot of beginners do and undercharge because you are scared to get rejected. If you are providing value to your clients you can charge a healthy fee without them having any reason to complain.

9. SCALING

There is only so much time in each day for you to provide your service to your clients and eventually as your business grows in clients and revenue you will reach a point where you feel like you are close to your working limit.

When you reach this point, it's time for you to hire someone to make your life easier and take over some aspect of your business. Whether you get them to help you provide your service to clients so you don't have to do all the work or you get them to focus on sales to grow the business you will eventually need to hire someone.

Let's imagine you are currently working 40 hours a week on your agency and you currently have 7 clients paying you £4500 a month in total. If you want your business to bring in more money each month, you are going to struggle to find the time to work with new clients without overworking yourself and burning out eventually. The whole point of starting an online business is to give yourself the freedom to live your life whilst also making a lot of money.

At this point or way before you found yourself working 40 hours a week you should be looking to hire someone reliable who can quickly learn your business model and systems and then jump on board for a monthly or 1 off fee.

You can hire an expert freelancer who is an expert in your niche from somewhere like Upwork, Freelancer or Fiverr and then just charge your clients more than the freelancers fee and you keep the profits. This way can be very profitable as you would be doing none of the work and still get paid a lot of money each month.

There are a few issues with doing it this way and hiring someone from around the world. You need to make sure the person you hire is actually an expert and is going to be able to consistently provide you with consistent results your clients will be happy with. They need to be easy to communicate with and fast with responses, as things can move fast in business and sometimes you need to make major changes at short notice.

Another thing to consider is that a lot of the time you get what you pay for with freelancers and you may be looking at some premium rates for a high quality service provider which may not leave you much room to profit from each client every month. Affordable freelancers are available but you will have to do your research and make sure you get a lot of proof and testimonials if possible.

Your next option and the option I have personally chosen is to hire somebody that you know who is able to show the right commitment and dedication to succeeding. If you can afford to pay them a flat rate each month while you are training them go for it but my business currently works slightly differently. In the future I may decide to use another approach but for now this is how I hired my first team member.

For many years I tried to get someone to be my business partner as there was always something missing in myself that was stopping me from finally starting a successful business. Every time I tried to partner with someone I always found myself doing all the work and in reality these people were doing it with me to see what happens without any real intention to commit and battle to make the business work. This meant I was constantly asking them to study or do some work and I would often be left disappointed.

It wasn't their fault they were not as motivated as me to be a laptop entrepreneur, it was always my dream and ideas and they were just along for the ride to show me support. But this taught me a valuable lesson for when it came to hiring someone to come into my business. You have to position yourself in a way that makes people feel lucky to get the opportunity to work with you.

Don't beg or pester anyone to come on board because you need "help" like I used to. Simply let them know you have an opportunity available for them to change their life and work from home because you are growing your business and then tell them to check out some courses or books you know a beginner would be able to digest.

The people that are serious about working for you and are likely to be a good candidate for your business are the ones that were so excited by your opportunity they complete all of the training materials and have lots of questions. If they are willingly studying your business and are keen to learn more from you, this is someone who is hungry to work for you.

At this stage you haven't hired them or offered them any payments so if they are willing to take time out of their day to learn as much as they can about your business this is a big deal because 99% of people will have excuses and you won't hear back from them for weeks because they were "too busy" to watch the course or read the book.

Once you have found that person who is dedicated to your business and wants to live the laptop lifestyle, it's time to start training them to make sure this is definitely what they want to do and if they would be a good fit for your business. I did this by scheduling multiple zoom calls with them over a few weeks where I recorded my screen and I showed them everything I do in the business while they asked questions and did some practical work themselves.

Once you feel they are at the stage where they understand how to provide your service at a very basic level you should now look to provide financial incentives as they have more than earned it if they have made it this far.

The 2 ways that I pay my team members are by giving them a percentage of the monthly fee I get from my established clients if I would like them to help me get results for specific clients, as 2 people focusing on something is likely to get better results than 1.

The second option that provides a huge incentive for your team is for them to start trying to get clients for your agency using your tested sales process. Then once they sign a client up you split the profits with them and you both work with that client to get results as they won't be able to deliver high level results on their own for at least a few months, depending on your industry. I have been running my agency for 2 years and I still have a lot of areas for improvement so your workers will always need to be working on improving.

Once they have brought a few clients on board and they have the experience and skills to manage your clients results on their own, you can then offer them a bigger percentage to run the account by themselves and you can take a nice cut for yourself and the business without doing any work.

I personally love this process, it incentivises your team to keep improving and keep pushing as the more they put into the business the faster they can go from 0 to making thousands every single month while also making you way more money than you could have made on your own.

If you pay your team well the work they do for you and the results you will see in the long term will be far greater than if you pay the bare minimum to a freelancer or friend and end up getting the bare minimum effort from your workers.

This hiring model allows you to hire multiple people quickly because you only pay them once they have shown they are dedicated, trained and have earned the company money by bringing in new clients. If you are paying out a consistent monthly fee your workers efforts will eventually drop down to the bare minimum level they can get away with to receive their pay each month. Incentivise your team to make themselves wealthy with your proven business model and watch how quickly your business will grow!

10. ADDITIONAL INCOME STREAMS

Once you have begun to scale your agency and you are earning at least £5000 a month from clients who you are getting consistent results for, you will want to take your systems and processes and turn them into products.

Not everyone who needs a service like the one you offer will be willing to hire an agency to manage it for them no matter how good your service is because they will prefer to do it themselves or keep their marketing in house with a small team.

Other people may have small businesses that currently cannot afford your service fees and would like to learn how they can do it for themselves until they can afford to hire you to do it for them.

Finally you will have people in your industry that would love to learn all the tips and tricks you have mastered while getting results for your clients.

All of the above people would benefit from a packaged step by step process showing them how to do what you do for themselves. Don't be afraid of revealing your secrets because these people were not going to use your services anyway so this is money you were not going to get if you didn't create content for them to learn from.

If you are scared that people will learn the skills that you teach them and create a rival agency to start stealing your customers you need to realise something. Most people will probably never take the required action to get to the level you are at, the ones that actually do will be far behind you in experience, so you will be able to crush the competition.

In reality though, there is more than enough money for everyone to succeed. There are over 1 million active Shopify stores in the world right now, so if after reading this book you decided that you wanted to copy my exact business model of email marketing for Shopify stores there's a great chance we will both be successful in 5 years from now so go for it!

You only need 1 client paying you £1000 a month to make the same as a minimum wage job. I currently manage more than 10 clients each month only working part time hours each week from my bedroom office.

The point I am trying to make is I am willing to show you my exact strategy to start your first online business because there is enough money for everyone to eat. This is why you have been able to buy this book with life changing information for just a few pounds, because I really want you to succeed.

When you are creating your content based around what you are now becoming an expert in, you should do everything in your power to help your customer get results and be successful. As I have already mentioned in previous chapters, the quicker people start to see results from your guides, ebooks, video courses and give you testimonials and reviews, the easier it will be to sell more products.

The amazing thing about creating digital products is you only need to do the work once and then you can continue to sell it for 100% profit margins month after month because it doesn't cost you anything but the time it takes to create in the beginning!

The goal is to take the skills you have and get maximum profit for the minimum amount of effort so you can continue to build and grind each day without burning out. If you want the freedom to travel the world and earn ridiculous amounts of money while still having time to enjoy life, you need to create digital products that will sell for you month after month.

While you are in the process of going from £0-5000 as you grow your business and improve your service skills you need to be writing down systems and processes that you use on a regular basis for yourself and your clients. Make a document that has your cold email script inside, make a document that has your client onboarding process written down step by step. Everything you do in your business you should be keeping track of on a regular basis so that it is easy to teach your staff members as well as your students who buy your courses and books.

I find the easiest way to keep track of everything in my business is through Google Drive. This allows me to create important spreadsheets and word documents as well as upload any important files and educational materials that me and my team may benefit from.

Once you have enough experience and systems in place that your business runs smoothly each day, it's time to start mapping out your online products into simple to understand chunks. As you see with this book it is broken down into a simple 10 step process that can take anyone, from a clueless beginner, to a successful agency owner in a short time frame.

The 4 week agency online training program then takes these steps and dives deep into the system, by showing you exactly how I managed to get my agency to the point it has reached today.

Once you have taken the course, you have the option to be coached by me 1 on 1. There is always something for someone to buy from depending on what stage of the customer journey they are currently in. You need to have different product tiers in your business once your business is established and you are looking to scale up.

CONCLUSION

You have now completed The 4 Week Agency ebook and have all the tools required to get started on your journey to becoming a successful agency owner in the next few months. This book was created as a guide to help you get started and understand the business models and systems you need to have in place to get results.

Unfortunately there is still a lot of information I would love to include in this book that I had to leave out because the book would end up being over 1000 pages long and you would need an entire year to master each step in the book. My goal is for you to get started as quickly as possible so you can make your first sale in the next 4 weeks, so I have kept this book as short as possible while keeping it filled with value.

If you are now motivated and ready to take action towards achieving your goals and starting your first wildly successful online business, I am offering you a fantastic opportunity to speed up the time it takes you to see results by offering a live training session once a month in 2021 to all readers of this book. In each live session we will focus on a key area of your business that everyone will be able to vote for in advance so I can prioritise the key struggles you are having each month instead of me just choosing random things to talk about.

You will also be able to ask me any questions you may have personally during the Q&A section at the end of every session. I am incredibly focused on helping 1000 people start their first online business without having to struggle like I did, so I will do everything I can to help you with any issues you have with your